I0756274

FINISHING LINE PRESS
www.finishinglinepress.com

Manan the Magnificent

poems

David Appelbaum

Finishing Line Press
Georgetown, Kentucky

Manan the Magnificent

For Kate

ISBN 979-8-89990-426-4 First Edition

ACKNOWLEDGMENTS

Much care in earlier versions of the collection belongs to Steve Clorfeine, Betty MacDonald, Sarah Wyman, and David Schell. My thanks go to each and all.

Publisher: Leah Huete de Maines
Editor: Christen Kincaid
Cover Art: Carole Forbes
Author Photo: Kate Hamilton
Cover Design: Elizabeth Maines McCleavy

Order online: www.finishinglinepress.com
also available on amazon.com

Author inquiries and mail orders:
Finishing Line Press
PO Box 1626
Georgetown, Kentucky 40324
USA

Contents

Aren't there annunciations
of one sort of another
in most lives?
—Denise Levertov

By Whale Cove

Brown leaves crispate
on salt-stricken potato plants
now dung-fired clay fists.

August. A noon sun
short on patience and shadow
focuses on heat.

Dust beneath is less soil
more a reactive element
unready to comply.

A girl watches from behind a tree.
She watches a long time
as leaves wilt, desiccated.
This is how you find feeling
when earth is let linger—
when leaves fall dead.

Evening

The end is when night comes.
Trees go to sleep
while the child dillydallies.

I want the wood thrush, he says.
I'm not tired.

Just listen a little
you will know, the mother thinks.

She was told that law is fixed,
sleep obeys shadows
across the child's face
It will bring quiet time,
when the meadow rustles, murmuring
thoughts of her unloved life
when night comes languidly
to rub itself against weariness
a wrap around her shoulders
to warm her walk about town
that sleeps undisturbed.

First life

From the base of the stairs
a young boy cries to a dark upper landing.
I'm scared. I can't sleep.
Words that he hears unspoken.

The father calls down, *Read.*
Breathe? the boy asks. *Read.*

Beside him, a toy bear
that can play Rule Britannia
a crumpled and tinny song.

Later in life, he remembers
the cold sheets, a flashlight,
but not the book. The musical
bear lost long before.

# # #

By the riverside they met
While the berme kept watch
over a rue-scented meadow.

They slept on her bed
that looked over an open stairwell
partly to show people
they were there
and wanted to be brunt of conversations
throughout the next day
since words were needed
to name their feelings.

They would be uttered by strangers
empty bottles kicked blindly
their passage home.

They tripped over clothes, bedside,
through moth holes in the blanket, they looked
at filtered gauzy morning light

that gave to each thing, deprived of form,
a lost memory of home.

Only when sun came
slanting in could he see
his felt hat flattened,
drowned in unknown liquid.

The small paper box
a reliquary where she kept
barrettes and her mother's necklace

each article arrayed in
its depression beside others,
even her prescription pills.

# # #

After, when coffee has lost its taste
when day has pulled them apart,
he is re-roofing a sheep pen,
deciding to skip tar paper—
too pricey at the lumberyard—
and unrolls asphalt shingles instead.

No one will know why
the roof leaks two winters from then.

The farmer will curse his bad luck
the hired handyman, but not the weather
that eats at life and ruins your hats.

You come to your senses
seeing in a dark time
after a choice already foregone

as though you had conjured
in a weak moment an absence
you didn't believe would affect you.

The garden

There's something I want to say to you.
All day he thinks this thought.
When evening comes with drinks, he forgets.

She returns to a house picked clean of words.
He shaves. It takes an hour for him
to recognize the man again.

The soil in their small garden
waits for him like a woman.
It washes his rough hands as they burrow
below roots, into sharp gravel.

Under a hot sun that entrusts them to one another,
he must sweat morning through
or else there would be only words
he has omitted saying. Instead, that grunt
augments the shovel's claim against rock.

Heated air wraps him in a strait jacket
as to keep his dread at bay
though earth in his palm stays cool.
But it refuses to let him tend its fertile roots.

He has knelt several hours, knees barked,
among wilting stalks that won't know harvest.

A breeze soughs. Then it is suddenly cold,
the sun, old and weak, is gone.
Earth has turned its back on him.

Now there are bonfires and putting by,
a finger on his lips to mute the mind.
Each day is spent owning his words'
sterile intentions that mark where love passed.

She fixes him bitter coffee for morning.
It leaves his mouth burned the whole day.

Fire

It is after dancing.
A bonfire under a canopy of rising embers
gives night back to itself.

A few cornstalks, splayed with roots that still cling
fume and smolder.

Snuffing fire is not all at once, in a breath,
but like an argument, can unrepentantly flare.

A defiant wind redirects smoke
to the farmer's eyes
so that he watches watery vapor trails
streak upwards to a striated sky.

When a tear falls into heated rocks
there is a cough
that is neither human nor mineral.

Once dull red, the rocks have cooled
to resume being gray inert things.
Early, they had promised transmutation.

In the heat, one exploded,
not a sharp, dismissive crack, but dull agreement
like a grunt of resignation.

What began as a circle ends a jumble,
rocks troubled and broken
submitting to fierce incandescence.

A mound of field grass, still sparking,
waits for the farmer's heel
to crush the resurgent beast
and become what fire yields, ash.

He has tended what was given—
to put an end to things
that otherwise resist unendingly.

But there are roots beneath
that crisscross a makeshift pyre—
these would have fire kept alive.

They refuse defeat, undying coals
that reignite this swath of field,
unconfined as wind or will.

It will be past dawn the next day
when people find whether he succeeded
or whether fire outlived its own death.

Bait

There will be potatoes.
My father laid tubers
under leaves moldering in spring thaw.

Now sleepless late summer
they are bait for the kill.

Small ones, voles, mice, marmots
feed, burrowing into fragrant humus.
They dig with lust under first blossoms.

Owls are hungry and in no mood
for evasion. They are swift like their rivals,
the fishers, and ever more prayerful.

Air holds secrets securely
as earth despite its love of show.

There is no moon to tell stories.

The wings are feathered so as to give
no whimper nor betray an absent victim.

Night air is pungent, filled
with promise of ripening.
At intervals, a thin shriek pierces
the folds of silence as life divides
in two, prey and predator.

Sometimes it persists, as potatoes have.
Sometimes it's longer—in case
a larger animal uncovers home with fledglings.

Pitch tells how the strike lands.
A short one means an owl found the throat.
A longer one, time for dismemberment.

I'm happy to be lying in bed, awake,
a single sheet over my body,
thought wrapped in broken images.

The remains lie under potato plants
where assassins finish their butchery.
I press my ears to the pillow.
Soft feathers block sound.

Scavengers are on patrol on late shift
so the young sun will find only
hapless rows of potatoes trembling
in a sea breeze, alone, unharmed.

Drought

Heat makes no comment
like a don walking into a meeting,
all become subject, stand at attention
a fist raised in a velvet glove.

Who would sow grass seed
on sand and expect a lawn to grow?

Fields provide dry mud cakes.
Children pry slabs loose
to build walls for their forts,
thatching a roof makeshift with brittle corn stalks.

Birds have finished mating,
roadside grasses are sere
killed with efficiency with weed-killer.

From air suffocating
its indictment of oblivion,
cries of innocent play escape
through a driftwood ridgepole

to tease, to contradict
earth in dress of drought.

A fine dust rises from the peak,
a pretend smoke, to augment their make-believe.
Even without knowing beauty,
it is jubilation:

hear cicadas' sober mid-day cadenza.

Anthill

To walk earth, on its crust or within
notch a line, an army on patrol,
each held by a stiff refusal
to veer separately, to see elsewise
impediments to life not yours
patterned by rote habit
without mercy from any gleanings,
angels bring light to those creatures
that fly amidst bright air
while in interstices below
only instinct, free of choice,
can awaken a vital impulse bound
in repetition—endless—without change.
We must stay armored, while you
turn at will from bivouac
to wander aimlessly, field after field,
in fear of earth, its terror
augmented by your absent love.
Should you open to your heart, death
will revere your gesture: patience,
a passage home, you will know
the awareness that evades you—
wanderer, you reject remorse
meant to purify you,
a breath through your pores
a grace from beyond.

A bouquet

It was on the wharf, miles from
ploughed fields where he first noticed her.
Coffee shop, bait store, post office.
On the dock, mid-thirties, diddling worms
or crayfish while she smoked.

He'd come for a whale sighting
(there was none), then stayed, watching
the silver hair, pretending to repair a weir
hung dry on the fishing boat hatch.

What she senses, she doesn't yet know
but her movement becomes more guarded
wary of reins in his imagination,
since her hope for strength is tied
to his being there, contained. In that way, he
belongs to her alone. The words he speaks, softly
with feeling held back, are ones she has placed
in his mind, as he would want it said,
a voice at hand to speak with strangers.

There would be summer days when she
notices his moving in shortened shadows
by the dry dock, and then to anticipate his look
in return. Then she took to wearing a long dress
her hair up, on one arm a wicker basket of flowers.
She would wait not long before their gazes crossed,
Soon after, she knew they would be lovers.

He is slow in response. In part, he wants
her separateness, to be slave to its force
that brings feelings out, holds sway
over his body so that when day's work is done
and rest advisable, it is her voice he imagines hearing.
Once she has let him be touched, she no longer
will wield that power.

He will turn away, irretrievably, behind walls
built to keep her purity, the way men are
when they enter into love. There she will become
someone whose voice he can't hear
but for words of reproach and failing,
someone whose life he will wonder
how once made him believe it was worth dying for.

Solitude

He is crooked as he limps
shoulders stooped so that women
don't look up when he enters the store.
Later he leaves without their eyes raising
to follow his tenacious walk home.

In the dark, the road is an alley
of stars reflected off windows.
There is laughter as couples pass through
words that would meet his ears
adroit with a longing to repeat them.
A sound of doors closing.

In mirth that turns silent, no one looks
at her shape on an unlit balcony
curled like a sprig of ivy on the wall.
Now he is free to listen and know
whereas before, for them, he had to be someone.

When he gets bored with town, he will
wander the fields, beyond the hill where
you can see the dock. In summer there are
fireflies. In winter, a shrill bark of foxes.

There used to be fiestas on the waterfront,
people, young and old, under moonlight
dancing, singing, before the herring ran out,
smoking shacks left to rats.

Then after, it too seemed silent.
Young ones found places
to be together, lying in field grass
that bordered the harbor overlook,
beyond where the bonfire turned dim.

As he sits against a tree, he imagines
their bodies naked, unmindful
of eyes that would find them concealed
in each others' skin.

Light

One light is on. His neighbor's, who runs
the store. Then one other, farther uphill
whose son is long gone to their herring weir.
Day by day, he watches this hour before dawn,
after dreams, reckoning demands of a clean slate,
long before he leaves his room for work.

Indoors, he can see the world open
the way he likes, an elongated stripe
of dark that rises, first above one house,
then a second. In weather it is different.
Winter blizzards make it impossible to know
which is on, spring rains bring
shape-shifting. Always his is a settled pleasure,
ceasing to be up alone, sentry of night.

In summer, sun drops behind
the foghorn tower, setting the island ablaze
under a then-dark sky. He can draw
blinds and wait for sleep, if it comes.

It is time of waiting.
Dark is not dark yet. There are sounds—
the petrels, the fox, the katydids—
still and as long as they are heard
he finds no peace.
Rest is the night, silent piety, solitude.

Only rain forgives.
It takes our words from us and returns our lives.
In its effects, rain promises nothing.

That is its purity.

Rainstorm

The sun didn't show this morning.
It stayed in a storm drain overnight.
The harbor, especially the bay, is unsure
it can exist underwater.

Onto thatched houses, it falls without sound.
Ours is metal, clanging drives thoughts
inward where they die in doubt,
each retelling a different story.

The night storm was efficient,
no bellows of wind to crush
garden seed intent on sprouting corn and squash,
just a clap on the roofing,
a tremor in the building on its sill logs,
an animal threatened by deluge.
Rain came again and again, repeating
the grate of repetition.
There is that faith.

Nothing of earth remains.
We must take to the ocean
alive now, in new form without a body,
no roots to tie us to name or place.

Night gleams around a candle.
Outside, sheets of water curtain the window.
There is no movement, no rest.

Home

A narrow hallway from which rooms branch,
four rooms, kitchen, bath, pantry, bedroom.
It's a single bed that draws him,
scent of vetiver mingles with sheets.
Life can be straightforward like that.
A door opens and you go through,
there are words, you touch
and let nothing else come between.
Or another door, where what waits
on the other side breeds unhappiness.
He doesn't choose but walks in
with an open pack of cigarettes and a glass.

The first toast is to the home.
The cast stove has bread baking,
fresh herbs arrayed on sideboard, from a neighbor,
his wife with their daughter bath time,
then story time, then a protracted good-night.
After, in good-omened quiet, she will
take the glass from his hand before closing
the bedroom door and putting on a record.
Bread will still be warm after.

Toasts continue, the door gapes and closes
with her on the other side, then gone
with the child and the vetiver.
Now almost vacant, their apartment is shrunken,
several rooms reduced to one single one.
There he finds himself, though at times imagining
being with another, a self who measures
how little space remains for living,
as if relation were a hallway
that needed you to close doors as you walked
until at the end there's the fire escape out,
and you don't know if it's locked…

Now he has toasted the devil. He's washed
dishes after breaking a bread pan,
and has swept the floor for glass splinters.

Outside, snow is deep. Life freezes.
Sometimes at night, on the sidewalk below,
a woman's voice calls out his name.
Sometimes, rustle of clothing
behind the closet curtain, otherwise nothing.

Groundhog

Things closest kept cannot be sensed
because there's no breathing room.
You can't make a map of touch
as if the inner skin of a tunnel.
Life presses in, not resisting,
each moment lacks memory
whereas human beings mix touch with pain
so as to desire relief.
We know how feeling shows love,
earth, its soil, rootlets, mycelium.
Underground, light's absence adds
a restraint to us that can perceive
a future while you live in what
is already done, sadness or grief,
what saints call disquiet.
Because we accept dark ground,
we have no fear of death—
an eternity, rest, comfort of stillness.
You who revere light must suffer
ruins, which is life on earth—
this dwelling, your very right to see.

Corn

Rows of corn promise little
in drought this summer, a waning hope
like the moon, throws crippled shadows.

He walks furrows, shade devours him
from behind while under light
a new spring raises from his step.
He now neither boy nor man
must sneak into the house like a child.

They'd decided to meet in a sheep shed
aware of each other since infancy.
Neither spoke when it was finally over.
There had been trust but no knowing.

After the ears ripened in fall rains,
bag after bag from field to farm stand
along with fruit and root crops.
Eventually it's too much and must be taken
to the town dump near the quarry hole.

Roadside on phone poles, crows wait.
Much is said but not for human ears.
It is enough to infer they are busy
with bounty, fighting raucously
brothers and sisters of one nest
even though there is more than can be eaten.

Soon will come time of nor'easters.
Wind sharpens its teeth on stones, the moon granting
each field's stubble a look of ruin.
Sound-effects to go, an uncanny shriek
mice make in jaws of a fox.

For the fox, nothing is out of the ordinary.
The earth always provides for its own.
Quarry is slow, plentiful. Pups will be fed.

There are roots rotting silently below
providence of next year's harvest.

In hollow passageways earthworms quarrel.

Dulse

On an island you can't walk a straight line for long.
Especially in fog, limits are tangible,
what's under your feet speaks to you.
If you don't listen, your boots get wet.

That's key to this place.
Either thinking you can walk
or refusing any outcome but cold feet:
the shallows are between
though you need just two inches of water to drown.

People come, so many crannies to visit,
life the way it used to be, slower, realer
more a practice for dying.
When they leave, so do their impressions.

On scattered rocks, pelts of seaweed cling.
They suck minerals from water and stone,
peeled off by storm, are restored in time,
they are moody, like light on waves.
To grub a living, you gather dulse to dry.
Look around and see how many driveways
make money the same way.

Since there's little else, young people leave.
New places offer work and the city
is faithful to its promise of industry.
Night turns into a time other than for sleep.

They return, their dreams of riches forgotten,
pockets empty, with little to blame but home life
pious Sunday dinners, the pathetic farmer's market.
Then they gather after dark, with beer
and music, behind the smoking shacks
happy to show new dances to their girlfriends.

Everyone knows a good time but when it's
over, the pull of mainland is stronger
the traffic, the crowds, the store windows

shiny surfaces that stir desire, free
just for looking—which is all you can do.

# # # #

In the shallows, there is ebb and flow.
In the deep, it's gone.
That's why I stay, dreams
don't take you away, like dulse
fastened onto rock, swaying in a neap tide.
It's the same all over, in the city
you're as moored to wind and water,
molded to a shape they put you to,
without say—

For me, the view is just right.
Sun is red when it rises, melting
mainland to a glassy rim, mirror to the bay.
By the front door, things are as you find them.
A spume of yellow light dissolves, water
turns gray, solid enough for fishing boats.
Day begins where it ends.

You can't walk without going in circles.
That's the law of the island.
You can't get lost. Even in deep woods
you can hear a background with waves
where they've been since time started.
They continue without a care for who listens.

Mist breathes itself out and in.
Brown dulse dries by grace of the sun.
Tomorrow evening it will be ready for market.
Where it was will be pressed down,
the weight of ocean does that.
When I check at noontide, you'd never guess
how it had been.

In the absence, songbirds sing.
Air has the smell of meadows warming.

The mother

There is no center to the island,
a concrete pier that angles seaward
passes for one.
On good days the ferry comes to dock.
It waits, emptying before reloading.
Usually, to load takes longer.

Beyond a massive pylon, a few benches wait
beside a boardwalk. In warm weather,
old people sit, listening for the boat
a low growl that anticipates it,
scattering their greetings on salt spray.
The fluency of the meadows doesn't reach this far.

Along the boardwalk, young couples arm in arm
walk slow circles to escape their boredom.
What you've seen once is the same
when you look a second time.

Mothers with small children in strollers
come in hopes of distraction—
young men at work on the fishing boats
have little regard for them
while their husbands are at the factory.
The hellos aren't enough to let them feel loved again.

In summer, there's reason to hope.
The ferry keeps to the timetable, the elders
tell stories they share once more,
which is why they've come,
the shipwreck, the car accident, the plane crash.
For the young men, the need to preen
is why the world is the way it is
even when there's faint hope of reward.

A young mother comes with her child every day.
They throw seashells into the water for hours.
the mother shows her daughter how things vanish.
There is no keep from the ocean

without paying first, so she lets the girl cry.
She is weary from getting up at night,
young men laugh with their joys, not at her.
Deep down the water evens misery out.

The pier poles hold thick crusts of barnacles.
In low tide, they glisten, wet in sunlight.
There is promise then the tide will lift all hulls,
the old ones feel it in their bones, but their thoughts
are fickle, unlike the barnacles, fixed
in place with calcine deposits.
To stop from ebbing, they retell the same story.

The cold comes and it is different.
Patience to sit and be still is worn.
A thin ice coats puddles on the pier
The young mother pushes the stroller through them,
leaving a wake of silvery shards,
but no one else comes to meet the ferry.
The rocks have spread over the fields
where earthworms inbreed below frozen earth.

There beneath is work on broken promises,
on false friendships, on lapsed times, on sorrow
that is as full as the hope-chest of joy,

it clasps the heart of stone, that it might become
flesh, that it may feel raw wind
blister lips and burn skin alive.

Conversation

There's a bounty on what you do
That means boredom is normal.
You lose count, kindling a quiet despair.

When she turned fifty, she walked backwards
longing to find where she'd come from,
footprints in fresh snow, lengthen hindsight
as she neared the end of the path.

She wasn't sold on life,
a pole bent like men she'd lived with.
That spry step still turned heads as she passed
a force like a secret scent meant only for you.
Her children would follow her—or not.
There were many beds on the island for them to sleep.

She is an easy match
ready to adapt to a man's tendencies,
his drink, meals he likes, his ambitions.
To move from one house to the next is simple,
street numbers don't differ that much
and no one keeps track of transitions.

What she owns she keeps in a small valise
left by a great aunt from the capital.
There is also a lamp she carries, home to home
that guards her seat at the kitchen table.

In her animal vitality, there is skill in
chopping firewood, weeding the garden,
thriving on house work, then swimming in the bay.
She lives immersed within her body, happy
for seeing things through men who keep her
without ever trying to make it better.
She could give less than herself.
It freed men to be a person they weren't.

Like water, she is shape of who holds her
absorbing his inner proclivities
so that his sorrow and his joy light her eyes,
a double of the man, in his likeness.

Then light fades and with the lamp, is gone.
Men are turned to stone, hearts unfeeling.
Their memory is gone too, rubbed to smoothness.
In her new home, she can speak of once living
dreams of a man she was with
the way he wanted it, minus her stubbornness.

What they miss is her ease with talk,
how her words lay out what they feel
but can't say, their impression
that went unnoticed until morning coffee
or an evening walk, when they interested her.
In her imagination, stories of their life
would find voice, purified of anger or resentment,
and they would listen as to Scheherazade.

Today she is trying to find where she started.
She needs to gather you together with her,
not as a pure past but a future to be born.

It could be an origin,
a sunbeam that breaks through storm clouds.
Her body radiates an irrepressible gleam,
lips pursed, ready to explain herself.

She motions to sit closer.
Listen, the secret is in plain view.

That was her discovery, walking backwards:
no reason ever again to doubt.

The doctor's office

His office was an old out building
beyond a maze of smoke sheds.
The side door let me in.
Later he said I would go blind.

Papers on his desk shuffled themselves
and seemed unsympathetic to me.
It is your own fault, they read.
You knew since birth, never took care.
I'm talking not just your eyes.
This is wholesale neglect, plain and simple,
your death wish leading you by the nose.

He was young, fresh out of school.
Wool suit in mid-August mug.
There was a procedure he mentioned
shifting to and fro while giving news.

Morning light, door ajar,
reflected on his diploma, onto
my mud-caked work boots. He eyed them
and then me, forefinger emphatic, wagging.

Rules of living are confusing to me.
No one said fix it if it breaks.
If my father had words, they died before he spoke.
After that, there wasn't anyone—
only the dumb world—who can trust that?

There must be a lamp that refuses light,
a world you know by absence.
You think you're alone, a ghost like others.
Ghosts don't hear, that sense is gone.
They're there but listening for escape.

Useless people are sent there.
Ones who know rules write the ticket
on a slip of paper and hand it to you,

As if it were for eye drops.
When the doctor reaches across,
he offers words also, it'll help with pain.

Outside I stuff it in a back pocket.
It will be lost until the next wash
when it will end as unreadable pulp.

He goes home to a clean apartment
to read or watch what there is to see.
There's a letter to write,
a cold meal, then silence at midnight
when his eyes see that they can't see.

Then he lies in bed, skin next to
the sheet, hearing night-time jabber,
only linen to keep him from his fear,
the first fear, of unforgiving dark.

He'll open his eyes come morning.
Terror will have been reduced to a dream
with feeling left from childhood,
once more noted in a black appointment book.

Living like that, your eyes start to go
when you're barely born, a drop of
silver nitrate, and the first time you stumble,
you pretend it was just a shadow.

Blind people dream in sound.

Fever

A streak of lightning dances on the wall.
It is otherwise black as beneath earth.
The boy feels he could reach across the room
and touch the far wall with a finger.

He is screaming. *I want her to stop*
I don't want to see her spinning.

When they come, the lamp on,
there is only a crack by the window
that's scored the plaster since time began.

After years, the momentum of memory eases,
the dance has stopped. A nightmare.
But fear of space collapsing
is suffocatingly real to him.

The two hadn't known before the party
that night would end on his mat.

A cicatrix of moon shines light enough
to shake sleep from their eyes
proof that the first time wasn't a dream,
his dance slippers beside the pillow
under her Island windbreaker,
one cuff charred from the fire pit,

glare now adding volume
to keep each object separate,
safely in place, no danger of slippage
so that in anguish of touch
he can feel how the far wall
won't be reduced to a tremor.

He holds sight gives each thing its due
to calm himself, despite wonder, no harm will come

from bearing an indelible trace
of how sensation found them, skin on skin,
a single mound of flesh, bloodied by her period.

The next day is work.
At the shop, rhythm effaces the night before.
His unfinished count earns him a dressing down
from the man who supervises.

As you hold one thing, another drifts away
separating effortlessly on contact.
At night as you fall asleep
the far wall is rolling nearer to crush you,
or worse, to open to infinity.

As if the boy had waited a lifetime to be lost
to the touch of himself.

Friend

I have steady work.
The fog horn gets me up before
herring gulls are done mewing on the ferry dock.
They are courting, *huoh-huoh-huoh*, by the time
I leave for the shack, morning light
tries to mop the shabby street.
It reminds me of the need to move on.

Inside, it's hard to see cutlery, only
slits between boards where smoke breathes out.
I stack one tray atop another
careful so as not to lose count.
Day is over at the hour the whistle blows.
In twilight, phantom shapes lead me home.
Lying on a mattress, I listen to steam rattling pipes.
It warns of what is in store.

When noise starts, I go to my friend's.
We listen to music on his radio
He likes country. If there's none, he finds a talk show.
It's amazing how many words people have.
Money, sex, and death. Sometimes love
but nothing's better than misery to share.

He tells me to get a plumber: I have lead pipes.
Maybe then, quiet would be more worrisome.
But it would be different.

After the last song, we stay listening to the hum.
It's strange what you hear then
someone's thoughts travel through your mind
living a life that isn't anyone's.

It can be hours that we sit like that.
When I walk back, the person I heard
stays in me, standing me tall and upright.

Morning comes and life is a promise
that night must have made to me.
The neighbors' houses gleam under new coats of paint.

His room waits for me.
He leaves a lamp on, to watch over
scenes that daylight lets in. At evening,
it will tell him it is same as before.

The plumber never came. But the room is silent.
Bed is cold, anxious for a body to warm it.
In spring, air will bring harbor smells.
If there's rain, you know when the tide is low.

I do what is expected. It's important to do so.
The other man's hands are folded on his lap.
I breathe a deep breath of sweet air.

Clothesline

Rain or shine, her dresses
hang on the clothesline, lofting, sinking
the way her life airs out, always washed,
folded, pressed flat, starched
as though their cleanliness brought pleasure
enough to sail through weeks on a breeze.
You learn stains aren't doomsday.
All manners of things can be made new again.

When we meet by the gate, we're bathed
in the smell of laundry soap.
Joys of washday have her humming
a jingle from some silly ad.

These are times of happiness,
clothespins lined all in a row, sheets
scraping freshly cut lawn, raising clippings,
wind enough to dry the load.
As if goodness, washed with care, could last forever.

Wind turns harsh, garments flap
on the horizontal, clothespins
must be plucked from muck
in too early dark. No longer dried
by a weak sun, dresses must be carried inside.
A wood rack, overburdened, stoops at the stove.

In snow that climaxes weeks of rain,
daylight is barely able to drain wash water
from bed sheets, hung rigid like cardboard.
When wind rises, they barely move
and when they do, it's with the deliberateness of a ship
that, plowing icy waters, leaves no wake.

What comes to pass is bereft of signs.
Sun rises with renewed energy, songbirds
nest in still-bare trees. Frozen earth
blooms puddles into which her sheets dip,
become logged, threaten to drag down the line.

This seems normal. Old people gather anew
to keep vigil for the ferry while young men load
in shirt sleeves without hats, hopeful
for some spice to which young blood aspires.

We're back in the atmosphere of her wash,
searching for our voices on winter mute.
They need special cues after weeks in isolation.

She has a new set of plastic pins.
In her hand they look like colored pencils.
On the clothesline, they make a rainbow
a spectrum from night dresses to tea towels.

Sheets are patched. Some skirts
have hems that sag, letting bright fabric show through.
Winter has a run to finish but she hangs a full load
that the young sun will never dry.

Stiffness is in her hands.
Wringing fabric, she feels a chill down her spine.
Her favorite house coat is in tatters.
Regardless, a wind will lift it into gray rain.
It will drape stove-side when she leaves for work.

Night Storm

Rain is drenching, stoking blue lightning, then black flies.
Hope won't bring warmth any quicker
although longing believes elsewise.
Clouds race low to sheer off treetops.
You can sense your cheeks lolling in moisture.
The real worry: the kitchen garden will wash away
with no season to restart a second.

The new moon. Pigs broke out
and rooted in a neighbor's lily bed
bulbs strewn the length of her drive.
It must be near springtime butchering.

A dead rosebush sways, wind
or who knows, maybe deer scratching their hides.
Green fuzz is yet to appear so it's all thorns
that crown a burrow where a fox dens.
A grail of blood from last night's kill.
The storm will do cleansing.

In a single string streetlights are misted
one or two windows remain lit.
Below, the dock has plunged into the murk.
The captain decided to abort the passage
and will stay the night with his wife.

Everyone has a place. Come morning
you see what's gone and what's new.
Land is patient for the sea's bounty,
to prove how steadfast are earth's moorings.

At night wind dispenses with sight.
Thunder returns mute intensities to fear
as it remembers threat of oblivion.

Tomorrow will be different. Shops
won't open, old men will huddle by fires.
We'll go out to survey the gifts—

lobster pots, buoys, a dead harbor porpoise
ten thousand periwinkles. Grace of the sea
but the world's is not grateful.

Road are swept clean. On puddles
clouds compete, scudding from one edge to another,
waterlogged, menacing. But sun is warm.

Why silence after a threat made good?
Fragrant air is no mistake,
to breathe it in, rejoice.
Gulls feel that rather than alluring surf.
They wander the dock like children
parading in salt spray rainbows.

At calm, the sea is a certainty
we can read in our bones.
But it rises from its bed
a mindless presence that effaces land.
an errant doubt.

Harvest

Tomatoes have a look of wealth,
corn is runty
but you can't pass on squash,
beautiful green-yellow, turban shaped
only succotash would be wanting—
life lacking an ingredient to bring it up to par.

If you pick over the ears, ripping
sheath to expose end kernels,
here and there is one free of cob borer.
Otherwise a brown mess, slimy to touch
like vomit, already chewed and digested.

Any real sustenance is consumed,
Potatoes were feasts for marmots
so you have bins of kohlrabi and beet,
kale, curly or flat, or hot peppers
anxious to heat your blood to a boil.
Herb gardens flourish, mint,
thyme or sage though basil is blighted.
Young men twirl bouquets, tied with yellow ribbons
for their sweethearts, who feign surprise at the largess.

At Saturday market, people buy jellies
from last year's berry crop, or periwinkles
beached after the big storm.
Eat them in the shell with toothpicks.
But the unnatural variety makes buyers anxious.
What happened to beans, six feet high on a vine,
or carrots, gnarled and lumpy, but crisp
so when you bite, you remember how earth
in its imperfection keeps hope a surprise.

Later, apples will fall, blighted and mealy.
Then, excruciatingly long nights with cold rain
to flood furrows between dead corn stalks.
Rivulets will flow once more.

You can buy books from the library lady
full of illustrations and leave still hungry.
People no longer are invited to Sunday dinner.
A calf stillborn: a time without mercy.

Strings of mussel shells rattle in wind,
hard from the northwest. A women selling woolens
speaks to a lone farmer, his dried fruits
saved from a previous harvest.
People from the mainland who come for souvenirs
have gone home. Alone you can watch
with coffee and ruminate over vacant stalls.

Sleet arrives, mingling with freezing rain.
The parking lot is treacherous but who cares?
Life as we know it is over. The earth is sealed off.
Layers of snow hibernate feeling.

I live on the second floor, above shops.
In wake of the storm, there are no tracks below.
Earth has taken back its bribery.
In its place, this whiteness unnerves us.

Life darkens into dreams.
Death wakes up in the light.

Milling frolic

Camp lights were colored
beads in old isinglass lanterns.
We strung a line of them along the front walk
flat enough for dancing.

On one side was the milling table
exactly right for six on a bench,
men on one side, women the other.
You never knew who'd be opposite.

People came, the point being to block the cloth.
It was called a frolic. Haze of cigarette smoke,
glasses of hard cider, we sang songs
in the old language. Though most didn't
understand a word, night was mirthful.
Your life unwrapped itself under the lamps
gave out its secrets, later on field grass or
on sand, a tang of salt or blood on your lips.

Wet fabric kneaded by a dozen hands,
wool stretched, made soft
to cling to shoulders and breasts—
music—sometimes a fiddle—changed us.
I was giddy by the time it came to dance.

When cloth was rolled to a cylinder
a spell came over us, a kind of madness.
we rose, singing, men apart from women,
one side moved helter-skelter toward the other,
without choosing, swaying together by chance,
colored lamps weaving shadows for a puppet show
letting us be playthings whirled by wind,
whatever you did had no consequences.

Dancing blended with dreams
you forgot and became someone else
your life lifted to midnight stars,
leaving a pulse to race in your ear.

I don't think there was an order to things.
We certainly weren't told but it was known.
A man would reach across the milling table
a shadow that shrouded the lamp light.
If you hesitated, it could mean things—
don't bother, try harder, not now, or give me time.
Also, you could turn away and be done with it.

When it felt iffy, you could reach in return,
knowing it wasn't heaven, but good enough
to wait until your skin prickled,
wanting to be touched, to dance,
to be led away from the colored lamps
onto soft, dark, dank field grass.
The touch stayed the rest of your life.

Scar

They said her father was a thief
but she couldn't believe
someone as strong and handsome
would do wrong—especially when
he showed off his muscles for her.
School children said she had no mother
that she'd come from her father's body
but she didn't believe them, he was thin,
she thought they were making up stories
to make her feel something bad.

He would disappear for days.
She couldn't bear their taunting,
it made her imagine being inside him
one day dropping out, into the world,
secretly so no one saw its strangeness.
She hid and became used to being alone,
the only one of her kind, with no one to trust.

She wondered whether her father felt that
when he went away—
they were alike in how they looked and acted
they might have been a single body.

She has never seen the place
she came from though there's a big scar
on his chest you saw when he went swimming.

When there's a reflection of herself,
she looks askance, eyes too close together
chin sharp, bony. Around the mouth
when she smiles, people say she looks just like him.

At night, under sheets, when she falls into herself,
her body leaves its shape on the mattress
she loves touching warm flesh.
She tries to picture how her father finds it,

whether his mind stays calm
unlike her body that obeys its own desire.
If it is dark, then no one will know.

In her airless room, there is a chill
up her spine. Her breath opens
a deep well, letting her feel the rush, falling,
re-gathering, as the moist surface finds her again,

blankets her until the blood quietens.
Then she pulls down the sky for a cover.

The neighbor

Each evening, light is more feeble.
It leaves my porch a little sooner
stroking memories of winter fires.

My neighbor walks his dog with a flashlight
once he's back from the factory.
The dog barks at shadows and needs calming.
It lifts a hind leg in front of the dead rose bush,
pauses as if weighing the reprimand.

There's barely light to register the change.
It is early for anxiety since the katydids
have started their seesaw chorus.

It's only because shadows engorge
and now swallow the garden's sodden furrows
that our greeting shortens to a few clipped words.

He's talking anyway but to the dog
whose whelp drowns the command to stop.
On leash, the dog looks guilty, but reason isn't working.
The man has to pull hard on the choke chain.

My neighbor is new to the island.
His whole life was a dream to live by the ocean.
As it would have it, he built upland,
a village house with its own well.
Destiny had a mind of its own.

The dog sniffs around a broken lobster pot.
Each winter the trap starts upright, on solid ground.
Then when the sun gains height, mud is all
and the wood frame is reclaimed by the earth.

His wife died in childbirth, undermining his hope.
This gentle autumn lets him believe
his fate has changed for the better.
An island protects you from the worst
like old bills come due.

By harvest time, his evening greeting is curt, stiff.
He's had enough of the insect din
that rivals thundering surf and rubs away
any expectation of relief.

Above the chimneys, the sky has curls of pink
where stove fires have been lit.
The dog is spooked by the widdershins.
It barks and snaps at the devil wind.

We watch as it examines the scattering leaves.
It knows the air will clear all inessential scents,
all that green abundance masks,
the intoxication of death.

I ask if my neighbor thinks of going back.
Never, he says, he didn't pay
for a return ticket.

The sea is different. Take a heavy rock
put it on the earth, and it changes things.
In time, it will be a memory.
Drop it at sea and it's gone in an instant.

The earth is a place to return to.
You can make a mistake and do it over.
At sea, you have a single chance, no more.
It speaks finality.

The dog is tired and lies on the path.
The moon is new, we watch stars
of the season to come light themselves,
dim on rising but intensifying.
Soon they will shine brilliant blue
above fields, deathless under heavy snow.

No one can be forced to stay, he says.
Death camp has gates open, waiting.
Guards don't shoot.
They know you'll turn after a while and come back.

Men

Light must be the sun's shadow.
It's crazy, the way it sears
waves to hasten banishing them.
Evening comes up an empty trough of truth.

The ceiling is low.
You leave height out when the sky's clear of clouds.
When a gale picks up, they dash
across land, skimming headtops.
Raising a hand would likely pierce them.

Noontime is cool under the firs,
cooler in the creek, where beer waits.
Men sit around, leaning against tree trunks.
A bottle gets passed, then a second.
They drink cautiously, knowing afternoon is ahead.

Some close their eyes and doze, supine.
In mottled light, some talk.
The way men speak, out of earshot of women.
Future is a rim of calm practicality
seamless in present comfort, in shade.
Steady as cicadas' monotonous drone.

This is the best part of the day.
They are a tribe, tattooed with dirt and sweat,
exuding physical strength in abundance.
A will they share that nothing can break.

Best is briefest. Too brief.
Empties are colleted, left by the water
they've splashed over hair and face.
If food remains, it's there for the foxes.

One or two steps out, sun meets them,
lording over scorched fields.
It's down from its zenith, kinder, blunter.

For men whose heads are lightened,
the rest is a game to see if you outlast
your stamina. It's over when shadows stop dancing.

Heat is not to be denied.
It burns hands as they grip hoes and rakes.
Yet like pure anger, it slowly loses its force.
You are different for having endured it.

Dusk is when bats flit overhead
devouring insects while the mind calculates tomorrow.
So many rows remain in fierce sun
before wicker baskets will be full.
It is knowable, therefore calming.

At home, in bed, heat hasn't left his body.
Sleep is elusive in din of silence.
A woman's damp skin presses nearer.
He dreams of shelter beneath the trees.

Return

This is now, the smell of earth
detained in a forgotten distance
that births youngest things, coltsfoot and trout lily,
there for laggards among weavings of roots.
Your nostrils will notice when a breeze lofts it,
chasing bees to shrubby buds not yet in bloom.
It is earth's timekeeper,
this hallowed fragrance, mist to sheer nothing.
When my mind is thankful, it returns to that.

It's a place I've never been to
white rock that glistens incandescent
spruce skirts its lowest rim, protecting
a beauty as ephemeral as aphid spit on cobwebs.
Once you're safe, you never want to leave.

But do.
It's a big event to stay for sunrise,
when the red ball lacks real heat
as it finds courage to part with the sea.
Like waves, my mind is inconstant.
It wants to go home when there is none.

The smallest scratch, a broken pellicle
releases the scent, returns me to awareness.
The sky would do a makeover.

Each time, its own aroma, hiding in repetition.
No matter if one morning were missed.
You could catch up with new arrivals
anemone and clover and spring vetch.
Smells are denser, more blended
since the entire meadow is impelled to announce itself.
In time, fruit trees with apples and pears.

Smoke from mill fires: that is summer.
It invades crevices between rocks
settling a dust on each blade.

A gentle breath can stir a windfall,
to rain on scruffy blueberry bushes.
The fruit itself will bear dust of life.

When you walk, that is what greets you.
You move ahead, it's the odor of work,
the rush to get done and outlive what's past,
pained desire rubbing out a savory
pitch of wild things that quietens
blood's yearning for conquest.

What brought me back? I couldn't say.
Constancy. But ones I knew were gone,
dead or to where we stare dumbly at night
across the bay, harbor lights, mainland,
or a fishing boat a late supper home.

People don't make a place
I smell earth first, the flowers,
the lie of beginning with no patina
no ash to deaden feeling, which is hope,
no stain of unwanted purity.

Meadows slope down to shore.
Scrambling among rocks for real dirt,
we can stand with one foot in each
but is there a place saved for us?
Land is a mountain peak crumbling within,
pebble after pebble, grain after grain.
Will it sink to rise again, under a moon
indifferent to life, or finally sink
drowned pod of seed, where we wait,
rubbed smooth of any respect for memory?

Where clouds gather above an unseen rift.

Theft

The boy filched grapes, mostly because
he was told not to. The old man
from another country planted a small arbor.
His father had taught him when he was small.
Bottles steamed and corks wetted to plunge.
One day vines were stripped clean of fruit.

Partly the boy was angry.
The man, who grew up with strange customs,
didn't want his daughter to play with him.
Now he has to mete out punishment.

As a man, he recalls his own petty thefts,
how stolen fruit did taste sweeter
with a spice that sin provided.
For young boys to seek
what their imaginations desire is normal
so the old man orders him to weed the vineyard.

The boy is stubborn. He likes the man, gruff voice
that sounds like a movie, but there's pride.
The grapes he ate for the man's daughter,
to show love that awakened his heart.
He wants to say that to be made to pay
would cheapen the deed and defile his ardor.

He is serious for the first time in his life.
The old man knows he's out of his depth.
Who says weeding would equalize things?
Besides, a memory persists, a girl
from a neighboring village, and stolen fruit
he justified because God meant their love to be.
But these vines and their grapes belong to him.
One day maybe, with this lesson, the boy
would learn a woman desires words of honor
above all things on this earth.

The old man relaxes when talk
of restitution is ended, and
the subject of the harvest festival comes up.
There will be music and dancing. . .

The boy just listens. He knows what he wants.
Though he likes the man, he has forbidden it
for reasons that confuse the boy.
Later as a man, he will know, but for now he resents
being scolded for his love and speaks back:
If he valued the grapes, why doesn't he
take the vines back to where they came from?

The words are spoken with passion. The old man
listens and because words would be a waste,
says, *do what I asked. That's all.*

Wine

My aunt made dandelion wine,
yellow sun-heads on sticky stems that ooze milk.
The crop came from our front lawn
and the wine was chartreuse in color, a trace
of heat indelible from summer and some herb
that conjured thoughts of spiced soups
whose aroma rose from hovels in the old world.

When she'd serve it, my mother said a prayer,
words in a foreign language that made us giggle.
There would be lobster with beach plums
if we'd scavenged the strand.
In dry summers, trees managed to grow pits
covered with a purple wrinkle for skin.
Then it was boiled crayfish, smell of the sea inside.

My aunt would open the wine. The cork
broke, she never mastered
how to seal it properly in the bottle.
A slight oily taste, it went straight to my head.

I try to make the wine for my wife.
She doesn't drink it—
only drinks wine that comes from a store
not a brew from weeds on our property.
When I get tipsy, she is angry.

She wants me to be like her father
who never drank and knew his way around
a big house—a simple thing.
You get up, sit all day behind a desk
come home at night with news of the city.
I found out early that my body
would be the one to work in fields or factory.
My mind isn't easy with ideas.

She thinks it's my job to get smarter,
meaning to talk about books or life
instead of worms in the tomatoes.

I don't explain, just dig and tend.
The earth teaches. I learn quickly,
Like making wine the first time I tried.
The smell, picking dandelion as a boy. . .

It wasn't always pins and needles.
My wife and I—there was desire.
Our hands constantly touching.

It's different now. She's all house work,
a few friends in a lonely place,
reading books that take her mind away.
The body forgets, you begin to see
how it's less devoted to you.

There are rough patches to work through,
you think you'll come out together,
if not, something else would work.

Winter is worst.
A grey mood comes over me.
With wine, I am mute.
It used to be best of times for us.
To linger all night, more our fingers
welcoming touch with the other's body.
An eloquence for secrets
that we'd never told ourselves
about commonest things.

The sun gone, then only fire light
until the grate held a few dull embers
that fell like shooting stars on the hearth stone.
Then, pure dark, arms holding each other,
bodies no longer straining for form. . .
mixing with our souls.
Night emptied silence into us.

Sometimes a real shooting star flashed
across the window lattice
like an arrow toward a far-off destiny,

in woodgrain, windwripple, crystal
in petal, leaf, moss and moon,
fossil and feather, blood, bone.

Floated seaward on the very word
we could steer by the stars
flesh and vision, some course
to avoid collision with night hawks.

A tree of nerves
breathing the wake of each other's breath.

Shadows

Leaves cannot hold and litter the ground.
Field grass turned straw in a nest for deer,
until it comes to dust, then atoms, then. . .

what of the emptiness, destructive vortex
that whirls no word with it?

Shadows at their shortest, sun supine,
indifferent to the thirst of earth
there spirit is.

Once beat with a vital pulse, now ash
that does not provide in advance
but springs only as hunger prompts
and the hunger of its young—
at a speed that numbs the mind.

Blessed, that which utters its being
straw of straw, stone of stone
for there spirit is.

An old woman at the window
in shade that grants a reprieve
watches a heat mirage stalk the meadow.

Can the name utter itself
in the tailspin of time
in the void itself?

Clean up

The last job, to burn the papers
ashes and dust, blessed be,
a hard shift as sun sinks into the bay.
But the word chose to become flesh
salt to the wound of a workday.

In the blur of flesh, he bows, baffled.

A single match, magic, and flames
lick the edges. They will be obedient
lambs to the staff of the shepherd
since they lack means of self-protection
neither rage nor claws
venom nor cunning.

With water to his back
and fire under his watch
you can't see him for fire's hunger

the force, the burn. With which
he would like to play
to lead with ribbons for delight

but may not bring in his house
because it would singe the roof
with its loftings.

What terror, alive by grace of the sun,
this fire too, lies concealed
in the strangest words: watch how smoke rises.

Both fires breathe only while there's fuel.
That there is an end is innocence,
is never in doubt. Smelling of ignorance.
All things face the same law.

The sun is to burn to a cinder
Then the work will be done.

Scarecrow

Without warning, spring nuzzles the soil,
infuses humus, aligns birdsong
with time and sprouts of jonquil, coltsfoot,
life that clears detritus of hope.

A scarecrow stands in a field, solitary.
Someone has painted a face
clownish, like a poster drawing
an infant that beams heavenward.
Crows are not yet aware.

Its grin is bitter-sweet
without remembrance of agony.
Heavy dew runs paint down the cheeks.
We who are shamefaced had looked
to be saved from ice, given bliss
for having imagined it.

That the artist won't re-make
time in a race during a dress change
in a single day, undone by the speed of what's next,
implies that we must protect
this perversely weak creature,

earth, under force of impermanence

must hold to our icy hearts
its nudgings in search of nutriture
the tremors of starvation

The decoy means to mislead
all in good spirit.
Schoolchildren will smile as they pass.

So it must be,
Let us try, if something human still
can shield you.

Hyacinths so redolent
groundhogs skirt their bent stalks.

Black rat snake

Clouds obey earth. Through a garret window
a young sun warms your spine,
flesh and vision, both inflict
ripples on your skin, on the innocent,
of hell by human hands.

To believe this final is insincere.
Is the word audible
in the din of malevolence?

Yet to be felt on the nape,
along striations feared
by deaf-mute dreamers: humans.

Fascination may lift the blind to light,
whose sibilance with a stutter is
felt by vibration in fibers of nerves
where an inward eye
sees sight and touch as one?

You play dead to awaken us, like law.

To shed our indolence, let us feel
all that imagination has wrought.

You are cloaked with a stain
that once projected,
begs release from feeling—
catalepsy is no option
for simple beings like ourselves.

Should you question, when you look
through our eyes before we strike,
when hunger stretches like young skin,
deathsong seems the advent of
new flesh, supple, lithe, a wholeness
you aspire to unknowingly—being human—
a dread and a bliss,
desert pilgrimage curiously open.

Grubs

Does the soul feel utopia
powers and angels, speaking animals,
oracles and pythoness
when your eye is altar for sun?
Pure radiance
should be blessing and joy.

Actuality is inverted.
In the great loneliness
the nature of body is to sense life
which below is presence
a harboring silence
that speaks without labels.

Above, what lies ahead, distance,
is nowhere, so the other is in doubt
unknown, unknowable
which destroys your peace.

You bind fear to words.
For us, lovers of dust,
to crawl in the sacred cell
sleep beneath, without epiphany,
whispering *Be*, beloved
threatened earth, *be*
as dust, gray become gold

not your searing luminescence,
forced from its innocence
but an ordinary place
a clump of damp soil

that you may hold in belief:
your word *acceptance* holds
common dust in holy sunlight
in the beam of vision.

Hut

No one would tell.
Being the only one who didn't know was unbearable.
People whispered where he came from—
his new brother couldn't have been in
his mother's stomach,
in candlelight she was a seal in bed. He suffered
taunts that supposed he'd believe their stories
because he grew up on a farm.

With two neighborhood girls, he built a hut
where a hill defended privacy.
Inside walls woven of branches,
no speech from their lips, dumb
with hunger from looking at God's work.
It filled them, lovers of making,
with breath pent-up, with dream and deed.

Their naked bodies hid them at first
then left naked to the world: new belief.
Hiding urged them to dance,
it was mania that frolicked
giddy along a sharp edge of panic.
He left in a shroud of solitude, exulting—
but the girls told their fathers.

He returned to the hut with a book.
Its cover showed two manikins
side by side, touching, a woman and a man.
It came from his father's bookshelf.
Long words under line drawings
confused him, his discovery, the blessing.

To imagine his parents' bodies
like the stick figures left a sick feeling.
Diagrams showed it easy to get wrong.
Maybe then you make a cow.

Once he saw a ram with horns
mount another sheep. When he asked,
his mother said they were *mating.*
The animals' thrustings were joined
to the word to impregnate the mystery.

Riding his bicycle he had a collision
with one girl and fell on her.
In great alarm, he ran home.
He would be whipped for mating.
His father was drinking after dinner,
every night with unseen comrades from the wars.
What war remained his secret,
best known when the bottle emptied.

The boy's words choked in his throat.
How to speak about his accident, making
a baby brother or sister? He had to.
It would come out of his body later.

Summer passed. With friends, he met
in moonlight, fields ample with corn.
The subject created divisions
since ones who knew wouldn't share
made up histories. The fact was
many details appeared only *in actu.*
Some bigger boys had deduced
beyond what books said. Many had older
sisters and brothers.

It was a criminal investigation
clues found and solutions tried.
Urgency grew among them.
He was not good at it.
One day a boy brought beer and he drank some.

Some of them would arrive quietly
then disperse—in pairs—each
to a crypt to finish the venture.

Afterward they sat throwing rocks at mice
that ran over bare feet. Every so often
one found its target and dark exploded
in a sublime shriek, grief or pleasure.
There was a girl he liked to sit beside
who would giggle, at a loss for words.

Night was pitch black as they walked back.
The foxes needed no light to find
dead mice, unhappy ones
that met somebody's dumb luck shot.
Better than a fox's gnashing teeth.

At home, his mother slept, a book
on her lap, coffee cup in one hand.
She looked at him, eyelids closed.
You know, she said, *your father and I*
watched shooting stars fall from the sky.

Smoke shack

They built in board and batten, leaving
space to let wind smoke the herring.
Summer sun added heat to burn
you suffocated until winter.
Then no draft enough to warm fingers.
On those days, you work to make the count
before the bell rings. Rare chance
for a cigarette outside, breathing by the sea.

The owners care less. The families—seven of them—
have properties around the island, big houses
bayside views. They want quotas met
if not, you'll look for work on the boats.
Countertops to be wiped, traps set each night.
Morning starts with rats' dead eyes staring at you.

I go straight through. Others need a break.
You hear neighbors' lives through the walls.
Why listen if you've lived the same life?
Yesterday's gossip is tomorrow's.
I'd be down under before anything new happens.

My wife warns me not to tempt fate.
She tolerates island life but misses
mainland gab, the family orchard, her sister.
Her fierceness at our wedding, young children
at play, gatherings for holiday.
Joy takes the old way. She wants to return.

She won't forget the apple trees.
Gray skeletons deep in snow,
owls' indolence, there spirit is.
Whiteness come spring, fierceness
as bees close around them: spirit.

She remembers migrant croppers
pup tents, rotting fruit
that dizzied yellow jackets to madness.

And cider, ambrosia down your throat
(unless outside a few days,
your head spun after a gulp).

Trees need workers, I say,
else the orchard benefits only deer.
Must pick, wash, grade and sell them.
Nature doesn't care what else happens.
The orchard's a beauty won't buy bread.
After a while, beauty will kill.

We left old lives behind, I tell her
and we're better for it. There's work here
and people to tell you what to do.
When something's wrong, they listen
for my advice—or let me suffer.
Because they plan to keep control,
they do what they can for the men.

It's a birth, starting over.
Though the owners won't let you in on things
they respect work that meets the quota.
Their lying isn't like unknown lies
that tie you to feeling poor.

In bed, my wife turns toward the wall.
Tonight there are tears, dry ones.
My own eyes sting, as in the orchard.
Apple trees are beautiful as ever they will be.
That will be true, longer than I live.

Old age

The suspense is gone, slowly,
strange, after years spent dying of suspense,
for the surprise ending mute.
Listen, eyes wide shut in confidence.
You never hear the silent scream.
before it's over, daylight outside
returns to where before it was.
Only a lonely shepherd looks up.

It can't be the dead don't.
they shake their heads at curiosity,
a short shot of recollection
something over high tea.

My neighbor's sick mother
when she goes to market to sell peas,
markets good character as well.

Sometimes she turns to the wall.
She imagines a crib, an infant
who laughs at shadow conjury,
dogs, a bark added to the show.
Then she can fly back to the tree of life
despite her body failing, despite
her mind weakened, spirit stills.

At home she keeps a good house.

What exactly did she say?
Words that were forgiving, that time
reclaims things once left behind,
a second chance to laugh like a girl.

It's not possible to not feel
the body suspended above blackness,
a dew drop is vapor in evening air
molecules destined for heaven.

Prayers of infancy, the only real kind,
pure sensation, pure breath.

Dawn's reluctance gives way
to clouds impressing cornfields
before they grow spacy over the bay
offering too much light for seeing
what you wanted kept out of sight.

A child, I ran in fields before sunrise,
a bird escaping to a dream
not caring where, only to stay aloft.
There was no future, no word for loneliness.
Later I learned the sacred wasn't mine.

I was a man like other men.

Tears rolled down my cheeks.
They weren't for the neighbor's mother
who took her place beneath the family stone.

I walked to market believing
earth exists, and each grain of sand
cradled a speck of holy light .

When it shines, I'm glad. When it is dark,
I turn on the light.

Sunset

It's a mirage that shimmers above smoke.
It doesn't burn but the now-dark sky
sets the man on fire.

Each night after work is a late task.
He scavenges paper, breaks crates apart,
forages driftwood. The owners require it.

The mess is live cinders now.
A glowing silhouette becomes a man again.
Taking no notice of transformation
he is impatient for home.

The sun might well be mirage.
Its presence warms to an extreme.
It persists until at night it dies, guttering.
He gives no thought and in daylight
walks on earth, unawares
but for an empty pit for a stomach.

But the sun doesn't die, neither
does earth. The man is mostly weary,
making sure things come to an end.
It's his way of knowing what he doesn't
know from the ashes.

Sun's work is done when his is.
The death is real, death he imagines
and cannot imagine, freefall forever.

Both sleep soundly, without mercy.

Meditation

Behind smoke sheds, behind the wharf
a man has gathered an unruly heap.

He pokes with a long metal goad.
When it pulls back, embers erupt,
stars shooting upward. Fire must be prodded
since paper is sinfully wet from skinning.
Fish smell made rancid in dew.
He wants to purify it to nothingness.

The best part is when it first catches.
Then he can feed its maw.
It's hungry when smoke goes straight up.
Its appetite lets him imagine an animal.

When it's out, he relaxes.
Praise the shadow, leap across the void.
That would have been too much life,
death of a livelihood.

Day ends in the same shadow,
earth ridden of chaff so grain can grow.
The sun has dropped, his murderous hand.
re-calibrates a neutral grip.

Ash-like, the sea glowers at the edges,
He throws the prod into the pyre.
A few cinders at the core mime
a violent closure but the fire is out.

A stray dog, night nuzzles the remains.

Keeping watch

It is haze, aura, dream
when earth first awakens—
the story told the infant.

Eyes wide, never sleep, it feels.
You will because I must, the mother says.

Sun too to earth says
it's night time: praise
flow and change, dreams must rise
dew must fall.

Because the infant sleeps,
mother must watch
so that child learns nothing
of dark sickliness in her mother,
barren formless birth.

When the infant wakes,
the ecstasy of names will lead her
astray from the other,
unknown, unknowable.

Loathing

Night is when he pretends winter,
burrows deep in heavy covers.
To see the mirror come morning
eyes buffeted from sleep.

He feels earth stands up for him,
listening skyward for an audible word
because of him that is required.

At work, he is wreathed in smoke,
it clogs his throat, can't be washed down.
The foreman has eyes like a fish:
He feels them on his back as he bends.
There is no word to catch the feeling.
Loathing demands one.

Smoke is earth mired in fire,
he becomes an animal that lives
solitary in a vacuum.
Earth as it shifts shape
unworks his love of fields.

He stoops, balance deserts him
he has to lie on the floor.
Earth reluctantly renames his body.

A beeline home as sun cajoles him.
while it keeps the heart at peace.
It is as lit as his temper. Lights
in the doorways walk him by.
Earth is a cinder.

He feels abandoned. Withdrawn, the word
from which spirit has been pressed.

Flood

The river's due to crest at dawn.
You can hear water climbing rocks
it normally respects.
Soon they will drown, along with the seeds.
Water will smother fields
and assault the farmhouse.

Pigs were rooting tomatoes yesterday.
One escaped, the pregnant sow.
We'll find entrails by the foxes' den.
They needn't tell our future, poor without her.

I hear water speaking, risen over bankful.

Winterkill borders, lace in flood time.
Apple trees: a carpet of felled blossoms
false harvest to follow frost.
Wafts of smoke escape the sheds.
No wash rids your mouth of the taste.

A girl watches from her bedroom, lingering.
Heavy-lidded, she's too excited for sleep.

Things have an order—you know what to do.
When you sleep, when you wake,
when you live, when you die.
Praise life between.
Water rises, you remember you're in prison.

Upstream, a tree must have fallen.
Bearing down, it knocks against stones,
sounding a death-knell,
grants the storm a muzzled voice.
The men will hear and bring lights
to show remembrance of earth.

A neighbor's lamp went on.
I knows it's always first.
streaked and striated in silver—
an icy heart, a shivering God.

The trunk is stuck, mute, in an eddy.
Pigs are grunting in mud
the way pigs do when they are happy.
Later they will miss their mother.
There will be no field to forage
it's underwater, young growth aborted.

Like a lover, earth does what it will,
with mercy, without.

Blindness

Sun takes its time,
one-eyed tramp in dawn's service.

The boy wants to know how it sees
with vision like the sun's.

For a few moment he stands
and looks, both eyes open wide.

He saw yellow patches, dripping down
febrile tears on a horizon.
Confused, he stumbles home, blind.
In that way he learns to obey limits.

His sees like an old man, but eyesight
is no prerequisite for sorting fish.
You need good legs and a dulled mind.
Besides he has come to ask for little
which exempts him from ordinary considerations.

Several mishaps at the fishery
and he's mopping ferry decks.
He sleeps in the cook's cabin below.
Hand rails lead him station to station.
He's known as *sweeper of the waves,*
a legend until you bump into him.

A hump-backed figure leans into a cigarette.
What he knows can only be sensed.
Others stay leery of his prudence
the way he moves in spasms and jerks.

He could do only what lacked focus
which he was unable to give.
What he attached importance to:
bed, a sense of solitude at night,
feeling apart from others.

There he has found someone else,
not another person but a self
that shuns intimacy as if myopia
felt like walls crushing him,
where heat gets trapped, stifling breath.

One night, at a cry for rescue
he was aware of having to prove his mettle.
Someone was overboard.
Without warning, he was first to volunteer.

Now he squats on deck, frozen
as sea water runs from his clothes.
Salt stings his eyes as light once did.
Sun dims, an other dark comes.
But blindness now marks a hero
welcomed with acclaim.

No one notices his retreat
even as he persists at his drudgery.

In other words, it is too late.

As though the sun whose choice it was
had already chosen you.

Sundog.

Names

There was a game children played.
They named it after the boy.
He hated that worse than mockery.

To play was simple. The object, to chase . . . him.
He ran as best he could, meadows, woods,
village, wharf, quarry, church yard.
Threat of pursuit wasn't his main fear.

He knew secret places. A foxhole in bramble.
Privy behind the church. Lighthouse tower.
He would wait until the mob passed or disassembled.
Outside would quiet.

Look at a face, you see a history.
Once it shows a knack for hiding, stories begin.

Later, past childhood games
people would stop talking when he walked by.
He felt they knew something about him
That he didn't know.

One time he heard about a magnifying glass.
After he found one, he set some excelsior
ablaze in the schoolhouse yard.
Men from town quickly extinguished it.

Whenever he felt people were accusing him,
he'd play on a wood flute he'd found.
In the strange way music conceals character,
fame he never sought found him.
He performed at church functions,
weddings, house parties—wherever people gathered.

A mask of shame lay beneath
one practiced of minstrel gaiety.
Even as society engulfed his life

he ran in sadness from its pursuit.
Where leaves blew against his window
he imagined stalkers throwing pebbles.

A woman stayed with him a while,
then another. The third was one-eyed, phthisic
with a passion for music.

He couldn't ask for a better friend.
She knew every quirk about him
and gave whatever he wanted.
He felt trapped by her care.
His days were spent on a small boat
that ferried between islands of the archipelago.

He came home to a cold supper
and silence thick enough to chew.

Public acclaim felt perverse. Its effect
was to drive him deeply into reverie,
'the way artists behave.'
Flashing a smile, then disappearance.

The thin woman sang with her guitar.
They were giving a concert for the mayor's
daughter whose birthday it was.
During dancing, he snuck out
to catch the ferry's last crossing.

It was a dark night. The bay was icy.
The last passenger who saw him
saw a man leaning far over the railing
for something dropped in the sea.

How could we tire of hope?
No trace of him was found.

The sea is a drug.
One dose and you lose faith.

The woman

In summer she slept in the barn loft.
She kept gardens weeded, beans and squash.
In winter gales, no one saw her until spring.

All day a dog howled. She listened
among the rows, sharing plants' anguish.
After work, she found it in a well, exhausted.
She prayed for strength to pull the animal out.

They became inseparable. The dog
keeps guard while the woman works the soil.
Earlier her eyes would refuse to look
when people saw her, now it is different.
She gazes where she likes.

Gossip that winter was an abandoned house,
off a road to the old rock quarry.
They said she was a phantom that haunted it.
Children would go to bed with
stories of what the ghost had done
to make them go to sleep.

Spring came without band fare.
Alder and willow wore fuzz, then leafed out
to rival spruce that knows no season.
She was never alone. The dog, grown mangy,
shadowed her shadow with its own.
It never barked.

The garden she'd tended went wild
as if distraction had granted
a free pass to dynasties of weeds.

Boys and girls, grown tired of stories,
threw rocks at windows after their parties.
Panes shattered, sashes scarred by near misses,
it became a figure of its reputation.
This was before a gale felled a tree.

Afterwards, certain of vacancy,
pairs would find an empty room,
naked bodies, no better place to hide.

The house wasn't the real target.
It was the woman, hair now gray and thin.
She's seldom seen, the dog with a visible limp
walks cautiously a few yards behind.

So when it burns, it is finished.
Ablaze, it roars magnificently,
gulping air like a beached whale
a forest of torches, feathers aflame.
Perhaps a candle a boy had brought
to impress someone he cared for.
When smoke clears, only sill logs remain.
Death makes room for living.

No luggage, she awaits the ferry,
blind dog in tow.

What fire devoured, charred matter fills
a carpentered square.
Little help for peace on earth.

David Appelbaum, founder of Codhill Press, has served time in the university as well as in publishing. Former editor of *Parabola Magazine*, he is the author of *Everyday Spirits* [SUNY Press], *notes on water* [Monkfish], and more recently, *Portuguese Sailor Boy* and *The Collector of Lapsed Times* [both, Black Spring Publishing Group].

www.ingramcontent.com/pod-product-compliance
Lightning Source LLC
LaVergne TN
LVHW090535110826
845146LV00003B/1104

9798899904264